I0063949

BROKER EXECUTIVE

Your Life Insurance Broker:
The Strategic Business Partner
You Didn't Know You Needed

Val Vogel, Jr., CLU, ChFC, MSW

No portions of this book should be construed as a definitive or fully-inclusive explanation of the policies, procedures, or plans of insurance companies, agents, or brokers. Guidance and suggestions are intended only as starting points for further discussion between readers and their insurance companies or agents/brokers. Examples have been modified and abridged to support the topical discussions and to protect the identities of individuals and companies.

There are great persons working at all levels and across all disciplines of the insurance and insurance brokerage industry. Any broad or general statements made that seem to the contrary are made solely for the purpose of simplifying concepts for faster reader comprehension.

Always consult professional legal or financial counsel prior to implementing a new strategy or purchasing a new financial product.

Cover design: © Jan Marshall jan.marshall@btinternet.com

Hand and compass image: © Starblue | Dreamstime.com

Back cover compass image: © Andreykuzmin | Dreamstime.com

Copyright © 2013 Val Vogel, Jr.

Published by AEC Stellar Publishing, Inc.

All rights reserved.

ISBN-10: 0989312828

ISBN-13: 978-0-9893128-2-0

Dedication

To my loving wife of 35+ years.

Michelle, thanks for being the true "strategic partner"
of my life's journey!

Acknowledgements

Thanks to the team of hardworking folks at Burns, Vogel and Associates. Your support and encouragement has been a tremendous enabler to the completion of this book.

Thanks to Jan Marshall for the exquisite cover design and unflinching support. Thanks to Heather Hebert for your outstanding editing efforts and guidance. And a hearty thanks to the AEC Stellar Publishing team, without whom this book would certainly not be a reality.

CONTENTS

Chapter 6: Use insurance to retain key personnel and protect your business
Strategies for using insurance to create loyalty and even "golden handcuffs" for your most crucial employees, and for mitigating the cost of losing them

Chapter 7: Turn your broker into a broker executive, or find one
The features of a broker executive, useful for identifying them or for molding your current broker into the executive team member you deserve

TO BUSINESS OWNERS AND EXECUTIVES

Is your life insurance broker already a part of your company's strategic planning process?

If not, the information you find in this book will move you to reconsider. A broker can be one of the least expensive and most valuable financial resources at your disposal. If selected and leveraged correctly, they can help minimize your cost, help you coordinate some of the most critical, yet overlooked, aspects of your business, and save you time and energy along the way.

The right broker can help you use products like life insurance as a strategic financial asset to benefit the long-term success of your business. They understand not only the changing intricacies of insurance policies, but the pitfalls of selecting the wrong products. And they are motivated to foster a long-term relationship with you, to continually ensure and improve the value they bring.

This book wasn't written to unravel the complex mysteries of the insurance multiverse. Rather, it focuses on a handful of key areas that you should consider talking to your broker about, gives you the tools to talk intelligently about them, and gives you guidance on defining and finding your company's **broker executive**.

Enjoy.

CHAPTER 1
Use insurance to enhance your company's Financial Fitness

Your business has seen challenges, and it will again. You might lose a big customer, take on a new business partner, or have a top executive leave due to illness. Expert employees will leave and need replacement. A bigger role on the next contract might mean taking on bigger risk. You will eventually need to transition your part of the business to others, and you'll want to protect your loved ones from any impact that might cause.

Financial Fitness is simply your company's ability to take on the inevitable challenges without breaking stride. It means being resilient and adaptable through periods of change. Mostly, it means being prepared.

"Financial Fitness is simply your company's ability to take on the inevitable challenges without breaking stride."

What many business owners fail to realize is the powerful impact that some forms of insurance can have on their plans and on their company's resilience. They have only met with specialized insurance agents and focused only on specific needs. But the right kind of broker, a **broker executive**, can offer much more.

Broker executives can help you move past empty insurance transactions. They are the experts that know where to find the most hazardous policy clauses, the least expensive products, and the loopholes you should know about. Broker executives understand the potential tax advantages to some executive bonus programs. They monitor policy deadlines you might not have known were coming. They have the knowledge and resources to ensure that your business falls into the right hands and transitions smoothly when you pass away. They can help you leverage and manage your insurance policies to yield the best long-term benefits at the lowest cost. And they can do all this at no direct cost to you since they are paid through the products they can offer.

Where broker executives add value

While individual brokers will each offer a different set of experiences and expertise, having a broker executive involved in certain elements of your business can dramatically change the outcome. Some types of insurance, like health and car insurance, are so widely used and purchased that their selection is a relatively simple matter. Broker executives focus on the less obvious ways insurance can be used to support and sustain your business. Insurance can be used for estate planning, retirement planning, life insurance, financial protection during long-term disability, long-term care insurance, and business continuity (or personal legacy) planning.

> *"Broker executives focus on the less obvious ways insurance can be used to support and sustain your business."*

To ensure your familiarity with these terms and to put the value of a broker executive into context, below are some brief explanations of each of these elements.

Estate Planning – Proper estate planning can save you money, potentially millions of dollars, that would otherwise vanish from the business value and overall estate you are working to leave to your family when you die. As a part of your team, broker executives understand how to protect your net worth and can help you put in place the best mechanisms to do so.

Retirement Planning – Many broker executives can also add value to your retirement plan design and implementation. They can help creatively protect your savings and control unforeseen costs.

Life Insurance - Life insurance can be one of the most flexible financial tools in your broker executive's toolbox. It can be used as collateral, estate protection, retirement funding, a benefit to help you retain key executives, and much more. Your broker executive will not only help you determine the amount you need, but monitor your account to identify, and potentially manage, any issues with the account benefits. Without

> *"Life insurance can be one of the most flexible financial tools in your broker executive's toolbox."*

proper monitoring, issues can arise after it's too late to do anything about them.

Long-Term Disability Insurance – Consider the financial impact of losing one of your top executives to injury. How much would it cost to replace them? What new business will be lost in their absence? A broker executive can put disability protection in place for them to protect their families and, for you, to protect the business. You can even use "carve out" plans for yourself and key executives as additional security for your business and leadership team.

Long-Term Care Insurance - Statistically speaking, seven out of ten people will need some form of long-term care during their lifetime, and many families are devastated by the impact of these expenses when they aren't covered by insurance. When purchased through your business, LTC insurance can have tax-deductible premiums, tax-free benefits, group discounts, and simple qualifications. It is also transferable to the employee and can be offered selectively to key individuals or to a group. Work with your broker executive to decide the best ways to use this extremely valuable tool. This is yet another area where you can create "carve out" plans that most employees do not receive. Your broker executive may include this kind of insurance in a "hybrid" product, which combines different types of benefits into a single policy.

Business Continuity – Without the right planning for business continuity, you could end up being business partners with the spouses of your current business partners. Or your spouse could suddenly be faced with having to negotiate their way out of the business you left behind. Broker executives can coordinate with your legal advisors a simple planning process to make sure that the right documents and a guaranteed source of cash are all in place to facilitate a smooth transition for your business.

Where to find broker executives

The truth is that you may already have one and don't know it. A broker executive is simply an insurance broker or advisor that has the knowledge, commitment, experience, and insight to help you prepare for some of the financial challenges your company will face. They have familiarity with multiple companies' products. They are independent from the pressures of having quotas or sales goals from an employer or insurance corporation. And, perhaps more importantly, they measure their success based on your long-term stability and satisfaction.

"... they measure their long-term success on your long-term stability and satisfaction."

If you don't already have one, you can find more detail on how to find a broker executive in Chapter 8. Additionally, Chapters 2 through 7 each include a list of questions to ask your broker and questions to expect from them. These are tools to help you verify your current broker is acting in your best interests or for guiding them to do so.

CHAPTER 2
Understand the basic process
a broker executive follows

Unfortunately for business owners and executives, the first response of some well-meaning brokers and insurance agents is to offer you a quote. The reason this is so standard is that many agents have a select, few policies that they understand well. They keep up with changes, understand their nuances, and can defend their strengths to customers.

When you call an insurance company directly, you should expect this kind of response. The agents there have only a few options to offer, and all of them come from that company. Their goal is to find out which of these policies you are willing to buy. Hopefully, they also want to determine which is best for you. But they are still only giving you an answer from a small set of options, when there are others available to you.

"... they will be looking to see what options are most appropriate for the goals you have in mind ...."

A broker executive's response to the same call will be much different. They will be listening for the goals you have in mind and trying to identify the options most appropriate for meeting those goals, despite your clear inclination to find a certain kind of insurance. They will ask you questions about your needs, circumstances, and goals to ascertain how, or if, they can help. They may even avoid giving a direct response until they can meet with you in person.

To give you a better sense of how the process should work, below are six steps that most broker executives go through with each of their business executive customers almost every time they identify a new insurance need. They include: (1) getting to know you, (2) helping you define your goals, (3) reviewing existing policies, (4) assessing your options, (5) executing the plan, and (6) monitoring your policies.

Step 1 – Get to know the customer

A broker executive will want to sit down and have a face-to-face discussion with you, perhaps your spouse, key leaders in your business or all of the above. There's a reason insurance brokers still exist in a world of fast quotes and faster money exchanges; and this first meeting, or series of meetings, is one of the most telling examples. Yes, you can get insurance online. Yes, every insurance broker will be happy to walk you through your options over the phone. But there's more to selecting insurance than going to a single provider and using their online tool to pick out the one that looks best, or cheapest, as you'll see throughout this book.

Think of this first meeting as one that might occur between a doctor and a patient. The doctor wants to determine how to help the patient, but he faces a vast sea of options to choose from when it comes to diagnosing and selecting an appropriate treatment. The doctor needs to ask questions to understand the underlying causes of your symptoms. True, you can look up the same symptoms on WebMD.com, but even there you'll find that the same symptoms can lead to a wide variety of problems.

In the same way, a broker executive needs to ask questions to understand how you weigh risk, consider alternatives, and prioritize. In order to analyze life insurance options, they need to understand what financial planning has been done, and whether any legal documents exist such as wills, trusts, deferred

"A broker executive will take the time to piece together the parts of your life story necessary to offer you the best set of options – ones based on your particular needs and values."

compensation plans, or buy-sell agreements. They need to understand if there is life or long-term care insurance already in place. A broker executive will take the time to piece together the parts of your life story necessary to offer you the best set of options – ones based on your particular needs and values.

Once a customer's specific circumstances are well understood, a good broker will be ready to help you move to the next step. This means helping you identify or refine the goals your insurance should accomplish.

Step 2 – Define your specific goals

After a broker executive understands you well enough, they will want to identify or help you define your specific goals for the insurance in terms of your short and long-term priorities. They want to understand the level of protection that makes sense

> *"... they want to understand the level of protection that makes sense for you and your budget ...."*

for you and your budget, and how to match that to financial needs your bank or your CPA may have helped you identify. Broker executives will often use sample options to give you a starting point.

While this may not be necessary for exceptionally insurance-savvy business owners, most need this to help them focus on the task at hand. Having options helps bring nebulous discussion about life goals into sharp relief. They beg the question, "What, exactly, do I want my insurance to do for me?"

To help you think about your goals, and the goals of your business, below are some real-life examples to consider.

- Keep the business in the family
- Transition the business to specific partners or key employees
- Boost my income after retirement
- Minimize short and long-term taxes

Step 3 – Review existing policies, plans and strategies

Once your goals are well understood, a broker executive will need to know what steps you've already taken toward them. They'll need to know whether and how your business and personal circumstances have changed since you last purchased insurance. This way, when they look at the policies you have, they can compare the benefits of those policies to the options they are considering for you. If your current policies have advantages over new ones, a broker executive will help you understand that, even if it means losing the sale.

"If your current policies have advantages over new ones, a broker executive will help you understand that, even if it means losing the sale."

In this phase of the process, your broker executive will request what are called "in-force illustrations" from your current insurance companies to get an accurate understanding of how they are performing and how much it is costing you. These illustrations include both minimal (guaranteed) and projected (based on current assumptions) figures. They can also tell you if the insurance may need to be converted from being term-limited to a more desirable, longer term, alternative. Gaining this detailed understanding of the policies you have in place will ensure they are accounted for in any options considered.

Step 4 – Determine the best option

Based on their understanding of you, your goals, and your existing policies, a broker executive will narrow down your list of options into the select few that make the most sense for you. They will focus on those companies that they believe provide the best quality service and have the most integrity. The options they present are likely to have clear differences between them, both in terms of drawbacks and benefits, and each may require thoughtful consideration on your part.

Unknown to most consumers is the amount of due diligence and discussion that goes into identifying all of the potential options for a business owner. Broker executives have a strong base of knowledge, of course, but they also participate in study groups and professional networks. They contact advance planning departments and leverage connections with other offices, agencies, and broker executives. They pull data from multiple companies and work to identify and compare the differentiating elements between them.

This effort can be considerable, and it's done before you've even begun to review specific options. But broker executives understand the importance of this step to you as a customer, and they have learned that the risk of a "no-sale" is far outweighed by the benefits that come with their customers' long-term satisfaction.

To present you with these sample options, brokers have to run illustrations. If you aren't familiar with them, an illustration is simply a quote for insurance based on tentative information they've collected. You may need to provide existing policy information, contract features important to you, budget restrictions, and an honest estimation of your health. Broker executives, in particular, will run as many illustrations as needed to identify the best possible set of solutions they have available.

Then, broker executives will present the results to you in a way that you and your team can clearly understand. The presentation could mean simply showing you the results of the illustrations and walking you through the mental gymnastics needed to compare them. Some may summarize the options into a single report or presentation. In either case, the best brokers will talk to their colleagues and staff about the results to ensure they are both understandable and inclusive. They will also highlight the advantages and disadvantages of each. Their ultimate goal is to help you see what options are on the table and begin making an informed decision about the direction you'd like the planning process to go.

If none of the alternatives make sense, it may be necessary to move back to defining your specific objectives. Don't hesitate to ask your broker to expand their search criteria in any direction you feel is needed.

Step 5 – Execute your plan

The paperwork and process for applying for any kind of insurance or financial product can be daunting, and one that many business owners simply do not have time for. The process for obtaining life insurance, for example, is much more than receiving a couple of quotes and choosing the best one. You may need to provide your company's financial information, complete an application, get a medical exam, respond to questions from an underwriter, undergo a background check, justify amounts of insurance being requested, and understand the results of the underwriting.

"The paperwork and process for applying for any kind of insurance or financial product can be a daunting task, and one that many business owners simply do not have time for."

Your broker executive will make this as easy as possible. They will answer any and all questions (or direct you straight to the person who can), coordinate with outside experts that you may need such as your CPA or doctor, and sometimes even provide pre-completed paperwork. Even if an offered policy doesn't meet your objectives, they will help you work through alternatives that could. They know which parts of the application don't apply to you, ways to present your financial information to streamline the process for the insurance companies, hints on how to best prepare for your medical exam, and even how to work with your doctor's office to get access to records in a timely manner.

Step 6 – Monitor Your Policies

Very few business owners or executives actively monitor their individual savings accounts, much less their insurance portfolio. The annual statements or similar communications can be difficult to understand, and it takes time to dig deep enough to see the anomalies you would be looking for. Also, because of their long-

"... because of their long-term nature, issues appear over the course of years instead of months..."

term nature, issues appear over the course of years instead of months, making them even harder to spot. Too often, these reports are placed in a pile and forgotten until a major problem occurs.

This is not an unusual circumstance for business owners. For a variety of reasons, they rarely have time set aside to review these issues. Fortunately, broker executives do have the time, and they will get your attention when it is required. And when it's not, they can provide you with periodic, summary-level updates and recommendations. To ensure your policies and plans are still adequate, for example, they may send you a few, simple questions to assess changes in your business (ownership, size, risk tolerance, etc.), and then use your response to provide you with recommendations.

It cannot be stressed enough that monitoring your insurance portfolio can save time and money for yourself, your family, and your business. Every business

> *"... monitoring your insurance portfolio can save time and money for yourself, your family, and your business."*

owner should set aside time, at least once a year (and more often, if needed), to discuss and review existing insurance contracts, strategies for saving, and the structure of retirement plans. Avoid the surprise of last-minute issues with your financial plans and ask your broker executive to set up these reviews for you.

QUESTIONS TO ASK YOUR BROKER:

- How many illustrations did you run before presenting me with these options?

- How much can I save if I get the improved rates?

- How long is my insurance rate guaranteed?

- Can billing continue to the company in the same way it does today? What information does my CPA need to know to accomplish this?

- What are my contingency plans if I can't get the insurance we're applying for?

- How often should we meet to review policies?

QUESTIONS YOUR BROKER SHOULD ASK:

- What are your priorities? In other words, what types of things do you consider when making major life decisions?

- Is this level of financial commitment affordable for you? Would a less expensive alternative improve your current quality of life enough to consider it?

- Have you shared all of your medical information?

- Do you have any special problems within the business or your family that need to be considered and/or addressed in this process?

- Do you have a file for illustrations, policies, and statements?

BROKER EXECUTIVE

NOTES

_____

_____

_____

_____

_____

_____

_____

_____

_____

_____

_____

_____

_____

_____

_____

_____

_____

_____

CHAPTER 3
The four most hazardous elements of your life insurance policy

The four policy elements discussed in this chapter should turn on a yellow light for your broker executive. They include ownership structure, beneficiary designation, collateral assignment, and conversion guarantees. They're easy to blaze through in an application process and even easier to forget about once the policy is in place. But they do matter, and without attention to these details, they can turn into problems later on. Broker executives spend too much time helping customers work through the results of poor decisions made years before. Read this short chapter and avoid making those costly mistakes.

Ownership Structure

The ownership structure of your policy is simply the person or entity that owns the insurance. The owner can be the person being insured, a company, a business partner or trust, a spouse, or even a joint ownership arrangement. Only the owner can obtain information or make changes to a policy. The hazard to watch for in an ownership structure is that the insured person, if they are not also the owner, will need the owner's permission for all policy changes.

A business owner named Walter was going through a divorce when the ownership of his policy was reviewed. Since both he and his wife were assigned as owners, neither was able to make a decision on the policy without the approval of the other. Walter disagreed with his wife's desire to keep the insurance in place, and paid for, by Walter. But a critical deadline passed during the lengthy debate, and neither of them was able to extend the insurance as originally planned, making the future cost of the policy unaffordable.

Some savvy business customers often ask about using a trust to own the policy for additional protection and control. The answer isn't always simple, but the two most likely reasons to consider a trust include 1) estate tax protection for businesses worth more than $5M and 2) insulation of a business from special legal or personal concerns (i.e. lawsuits or a child that needs special care). Discuss with your broker executive your particular circumstance to see if the time and money needed to set up the trust is cost effective in the long-term.

Another important consideration in policy ownership is buy-sell or business continuation planning (More on this is included in Chapter 5). It may be beneficial for the company to own the insurance policies, for business partners to own insurance on one another, or even to set up a new LLC to own the policies.

Discuss with your broker executive the options best suited to you and your business. Don't assume one type of ownership is better than another until it's been carefully reviewed and compared. It's better to set it up correctly the first time than to spend a lot of time and money fixing it later.

Beneficiary Designation

At the other end of an insurance lifecycle is the beneficiary, the one that receives the benefit when the insured dies. You can use the beneficiary structure to insure your business against the loss of key personnel, your bank against your default on a loan, or your family against the loss of your income. The death of a significant person in our lives is never easy, but receiving life insurance benefits that are both tax-free and not subject to a probate process can ease the burden

"You can use the beneficiary structure to insure your business against the loss of key personnel, your bank against your default on a loan, or your family against the loss of your income."

during this difficult time.

With creative planning comes room for error. Owners may name the bank as the sole beneficiary, despite the fact that the death benefit is more than the amount of the loan. Sometimes an estate is left as the beneficiary, creating issues such as unnecessary taxation, probate expenses, or delays in receiving benefits. Individual policy holders often forget to change the beneficiary after the death of a spouse, a divorce, or a change in relationship status.

As your life and your business circumstances change over time, as they inevitably will, it's important to revisit and review this aspect of your insurance. Your broker executive will help you verify and understand your current beneficiary designations and suggest changes when appropriate.

Collateral Assignment

Collateral assignment is typically the use of life insurance as collateral for a loan. This may be a smart move, and it's one your broker executive can help guide you through and even expedite. But it's also an area where business owners often move too quickly because they're in a hurry to receive the funds. Three common mistakes business owners make here are: (1) taking out new insurance when existing policies would suffice, (2) assigning the lender as the sole beneficiary for a new policy, and (3) purchasing more insurance than is necessary to cover the loan.

> *"Three common mistakes business owners make here are:*
> *(1) taking out new insurance when existing policies would suffice,*
> *(2) assigning the lender as the sole beneficiary for a new policy, and*
> *(3) purchasing more insurance than is necessary for the loan."*

A complex collateral assignment issue arose during discussions to finalize a Buy-Sell Agreement for a company. The business had three owners, each with their own Term Life insurance policy – adding up to a total benefit of $6M. Their policy benefits had been assigned to their bank as collateral for a loan, with the condition that the entire loan balance be paid if any of the three passed away. Fortunately, the owners made the right decision to discuss the matter with their broker, their attorneys and their CPA. As a part of the team of advisors, the broker executive made sure all of the parties worked with accurate information, brought in a specialized legal consultant to assist, and put forth a myriad of options for them to consider. The owners elected to apply for new insurance and to assign to the bank only one third of the benefit from each owner. The new assignment was set up with an ATIMA (As Their Interest May Appear) clause to ensure only the loan balance was covered. This helped the business, and their families, dodge what would have been a devastating financial blow if one of them had died.

When considering options for life insurance as collateral, be sure to review your existing policies with your broker to determine whether additional insurance is needed or if the debt can be covered simply by adding the bank as an assignee. If you are using a personal policy for the loan, make sure family members are still beneficiaries and that the remainder of the benefit is allocated to them after the bank debt has been paid. Be open and transparent with your broker executive, and they'll help you get what you need.

"Be open and transparent with your broker executive, and they'll help you get what you need."

You may be more comfortable with a separate insurance policy to cover the business debt to avoid touching the one designated for your family. Many business owners do this, and simply ask their broker to make the bank the assignee for the policy. This can work well, provided you leave yourself wiggle room. For one thing, the bank will only require an ATIMA reimbursement (the remainder of the loan) if you die.

Be sure to designate another beneficiary to this policy upfront, perhaps the business itself, to avoid the red tape associated with trying to add a beneficiary later.

Conversion Guarantees:

For Term Life, or life insurance defined by a fixed timeline of guaranteed coverage, there is one deadline almost as important as the end date of the contract itself. That is the conversion deadline. If you've already purchased a Term Life policy, one of the selling points for you was most likely the ability to convert that insurance into Cash Value Life insurance later. You probably purchased the insurance when you were in good health and therefore received a "preferred" status. Conversion options allow you to obtain cash value insurance at the original rate class without taking a new medical exam or answering any medical questions. We all understand the potential for health problems to develop as we get older, and we want to be prepared. But it can be all for nothing if no one remembers to capitalize on this benefit by changing it to long-term coverage prior to the policy's conversion deadline.

Consider that there are many types of term conversions available. Some policies must be converted at a specified age (such as 65 or 75), and some have limits in years (such as 10 or 15 years). Some have special rules that guide the conversion deadline, including that the conversion take place prior to the last year of the guaranteed term period. Only the most proactive and experienced brokers will be actively monitoring all of their customers' policies.

Another pitfall to watch for in your policy is contract language loopholes that apply to automatic conversion guarantees. As companies adapt to market pressures to reduce price, they may use contract language to allow them to limit the benefit of the conversion without you being aware of it. One example is the use of "blending" insurance types to offer an increased benefit such as Term Life that eventually converts into Cash Value Life. This makes sense in some cases, but the benefits of this blend can rely heavily on the successful management and earnings of the insurance company holding your contract. Another example is the cost of term-limited riders attached to your primary policy. If riders like this aren't converted or removed, their often hidden cost can become exorbitant and impact your primary coverage.

There are even some conversion guarantees that require you to convert to a very specific type of insurance policy. The optimal conversion options give you a choice from a range of permanent policies at your original "health classification." Keep in mind that guarantees are based on the claims-paying ability of the issuing insurance company.

The bottom line is to make sure your broker executive is aware of these critical nuances and is actively helping you manage them. Take the time to meet with them to review your insurance portfolio regularly. Don't put off responding to your broker until it's too late to convert. Know your conversion deadline and add it to your personal list of events to watch for. Remember that there's no need to wait until the conversion date to make your insurance permanent. Conversions can provide a real benefit, when set up correctly and timed carefully.

> *"... make sure your broker executive is aware of these critical nuances and is actively helping you manage them."*

QUESTIONS TO ASK YOUR BROKER:

- What kind of policy ownership structure will be the most flexible later on while still accomplishing my goals?

- Would it make sense for me to consider having a trust be the owner of my policies?

- Are these beneficiaries the best ones for me? When should I check them again?

- Can I use an existing insurance policy for my loan collateral and still protect my family?

- If I make the bank my beneficiary, will they need to approve any changes to the beneficiary later?

- I'm getting insurance to cover a bank loan – is this the lowest cost choice available anywhere?

- When, exactly, is the last date or age that I can convert this Term Life policy?

- Are there any other restrictions to my conversion option to be aware of?

- How will I be notified when my conversion deadline is approaching?

QUESTIONS YOUR BROKER SHOULD ASK:

- Do you understand the limitations created when your insurance policy is owned by someone else?

- Do you have any insurance policies in place that we should review? Has your health or medicine intake changed much since you bought your last insurance?

- Are you using this insurance only as collateral for a loan, or do you also need it to protect your family or your business?

- If you reduce the amount of coverage for your family or business for this loan, will the remainder be enough to cover their needs?

- How far in advance of your conversion date would you like me to contact you to ensure we change the term insurance into a cash value insurance policy?

NOTES

CHAPTER 4
Five reviews associated with
proactive policy administration

The sea of insurance options and financial strategies is dynamic, and the livelihood of a broker executive is based on understanding this environment. They are in the best position to detect problems in your existing policies and to understand how changes in the external insurance environment could impact you. They know where to look for the most common pitfalls and when to open up your policy to check for them.

Five of the most common components of proactive service to expect from a broker executive are covered below. These include: Ownership Structure Reviews, Beneficiary Designation Reviews, Review and Notification of Conversion Deadlines, Policy Reviews, and Better Contract Availability. The first two of these were also discussed in Chapter 3 as hazardous policy elements, and they are also included here to give you a complete picture of ways those hazards can be mitigated before they occur.

Ownership Structure Reviews

A broker executive will generally review your ownership structure as a part of any review, either with you or as a part of their normal operation. However, when a change is needed, there may be sensitive and complex issues to overcome. Your broker could discover that a bank owns the insurance when the business should. A business may own the insurance when a Trust should have been set up. The business is the owner but has changed names. Spouses may own insurance on one another, making it difficult to unravel if a divorce occurs. Even when a change is ideal, policy nuances like collateral assignments may limit or complicate the process.

These subtleties and potential issues are compounded by the fact that most brokers assume the owner originally selected is still the correct person or entity. Some agents may simply be happy with the sale and inadvertently take this kind of detail for granted. It should come up in discussion during routine questions about your needs. Policy ownership is clearly designated on the application, but it is seldom noticed for the impact it could have on a business or family.

Beneficiary Designation Reviews

It is also important to periodically review your primary and contingent beneficiary designations. Your broker executive will recognize this, as they should have during the initial application process, and make sure it's considered appropriately. This isn't a massive undertaking for you, but as life happens your beneficiaries may need to be changed. There are often policies that have an ex-spouse or ex-partner designated as the beneficiary that needs to be updated. Business partners or even the business itself may have changed and should no longer be listed. When the business is a beneficiary, it may be appropriate to change it to a family member or trust and to use a collateral assignment to meet your business obligations.

Few policy owners or even brokers take the time to ask questions about beneficiaries on their previous contracts, even though they can and do need to change periodically. Once identified, the fix is often as simple as a Change of Beneficiary form. If you have a broker executive, you can expect them to facilitate this process to make sure your policies will deliver the benefits you're paying for.

Review and Notification of Conversion Deadlines

A broker executive will typically have reminders set to contact you prior to your policy or rider conversion deadlines. They understand the importance of this date and will be watching for it. They will likely contact you several months in advance of the final date to ensure they have enough time to reach you and to help you consider your options carefully.

In a recent example, a customer named Janet was contacted to let her know that her conversion date was coming up, even though there were five years left in her Term Life policy. After comparing her conversion options with new policy considerations, she decided that the low rate she was currently paying was more important to her than the longer term savings.

In another case, Bradley, an active and health-conscious business owner, was considering his conversion deadline. Since his health had improved from when he originally purchased his Term Life plan, the recommendation he received was to apply for new coverage. Because of his improved health, he received a "preferred" status and a reduced premium. This option was therefore more economical than his conversion price, and it gave him the option to convert at a future date at the new rate class.

The point is for you to have the *opportunity* and the

information to make the best decision for yourself. If you aren't given the decision to make, your options may become extremely limited. You could be forced to retake medical exams that place you in a higher cost category, for example. When that occurs, it's likely your payments will increase.

Policy Reviews

When you bought your life insurance policy, you understood there would be certain benefits. What you may not realize is how these benefits can be impacted by other factors. So, how do you know if your contract will deliver what you expect?

Many insurance brokers will commit to monitoring your policy. Broker executives will go further, taking the time to review your annual statements and other reports and to discuss them with you, particularly when they find issues. Some of these problems may take years to become obvious. But it's important to know they exist as soon as they can be detected.

"Broker executives will go further, taking the time to review your annual statements and other reports and to discuss them with you, particularly when they find issues."

In a recent case for a large business firm, the business purchased cash value life insurance to fund a deferred compensation plan for its key executives. The plan was designed to supplement their retirement income with roughly $500K to each executive. When the first executive retired, the cash value of the insurance was only enough to cover half of the benefit that had been promised. Since the business was still committed to providing the supplemental retirement to the employee, the unfunded half ($250K) had to be paid directly out of company accounts. Although the business was fortunate to have some cash value to use, this is a significant impact even for a large business, and one that could have been mitigated by additional funding.

Your life insurance policy may also have addendums, or "riders," that need to be reviewed. Riders are often purchased as a way to provide additional benefits such as insurance for your spouse and children, or even Long Term Care benefits. However, the cost of riders

> *"Your life insurance policy may also have addendums, or 'riders,' that need to be reviewed."*

may increase over time and negatively impact the cash value in your life insurance policy. They may also have their own conversion deadlines and restrictions.

To understand your policy's specific benefits, your broker executive will most likely use what are known as In-Force Illustrations. These come from the insurance company, and they give the details of policies you have in place and their benefits over time. Your broker should typically work on your behalf to obtain this information. However, if you aren't already being presented with this information, you can obtain much of it yourself by calling your insurance company's client services department and requesting time with your broker to better understand your findings.

Better Contract Availability

So, how do you know you have the best policy? If a better one is available, how difficult is it to change?

While this is partly a subjective response, the best contract is the one that gives you near term comfort and long term protection. The best policy for you will change depending on the time of your life, the success of your business, your current (and future) health, and other similar pressures. It also depends on the current suite of offerings coming from insurance companies, which regularly change based on their own economic pressures.

> *"... the best policy is the one that gives you near term comfort and long term protection."*

Work closely with a broker executive to make the best decision you can up-front, and then be sure to contact them (or take their calls) every year or so. This is especially important if a change has occurred that might impact your insurance. This could be a new diet that's changed your health conditions for the better, a change in marital status, or significant changes in your business size. Reviews of existing versus new policies never hurt, and new options are often coming available that might be even better.

QUESTIONS TO ASK YOUR BROKER:

- What kind of statements will I get from you and/or from the companies we are insured with?

- Is there any additional cost to me for an annual or bi-annual review?

- Is there any risk associated with my current ownership structure?

- Are these the right beneficiaries?

- What's the difference between the conversion deadline and the expiration date for my Term Life policy?

- Can you give me a summary of my policies and how well they are performing?

- Are there any other policies out there that would give me the same, or better, results for less cost?

QUESTIONS YOUR BROKER SHOULD ASK:

- Have you listed contingent beneficiaries on all of your policies? When were they last reviewed?

- Have you had any life-changing events such as a divorce, the birth of a child, or a death in your family?

- Is your health better or worse than it was when you first applied for life insurance?

- Has your business experienced any dramatic growth or shrinkage in the last couple of years?

- What kind of policies do you have in place today, either for yourself, your business, or any of your key executives?

- Have any of your goals or objectives for using insurance changed since you first purchased your plans?

- Do you mind if I contact you annually to review your policies and their future benefits?

NOTES

CHAPTER 5
Make sure your company will fall into the right hands

This may be a hard question to think about, but who gets the business after you pass away? Is it a family member, an executive board, a co-owner, a trust? Will you have an increased share in the business if another owner passes away, or will their spouse have to manage their portion? Is everything set up to transition smoothly, and is that cost covered in your business models?

Many of these questions can be resolved through careful succession planning. Make sure you have a broker executive on your executive team. Work with them to think through your objectives and what you need to put in place to accomplish them. Leverage their experience to ensure a smooth transition for your family, your business partners, and yourself.

Four key elements of succession planning include: identifying objectives, communication and preparation, transition funding, and documentation.

Identifying Objectives

First, sit down with your broker executive and walk through the scenario of a final fire drill. Review the questions at the start of the chapter and any specific concerns you have. Keep in mind any existing policies or legal documents, including your buy-sell agreement for your business. The following are examples of objectives you may need to consider:

- Compensation plans or payments that will be owed to survivors
- Protection plans for family and business partners
- Protection plans to ensure continuity of business operations
- Business legacy constraints that need to be addressed
- Funding sources to pay for a succession, if any are already in place

Communication and Preparation

Once you've worked through the issues above, and this may take some time, you'll need to communicate your plan to your family and coworkers. Your broker executive will likely offer help in this regard, but the responsibility to communicate with those who could be affected is primarily yours. Share your objectives, let them know your intentions, and answer any questions they have. Lay out clear plans for how you expect your family to be taken care of and what you expect it to cost. Seek to understand their concerns and assure them that your executive team is ready to protect your legacy and to support your plan. Being open and honest in this part of the process is difficult, but it can also be incredibly helpful later on in laying out how things need to be handled.

Above all, put together a logical and clearly understood plan that has been discussed and is well-understood by company management and family members. Save them the time, effort, and stress of trying to work through it later.

Transition Funding

It should come as no surprise that money will be needed when you pass away. Your successor will need funding to cover the purchase-sale of stock in the company and for any training, hiring, or other transition costs. The best laid plans are pointless without the funds to implement them.

Of course, there are a number of ways to save money for rainy days, but life insurance was specially designed for this circumstance. Many only think of life insurance as a way to cover their family's future needs, but it's much more than that. It provides an income tax-free benefit precisely when it is most needed. It can even be structured to avoid inclusion in your estate. Your broker executive will know this, as it's one of their specialties, so help connect the dots between your life insurance plans and your succession strategy. Make sure it's enough to meet your needs.

Documentation

Equally as important as defining your plan and ensuring the funding is there to implement it are the legal documents you'll need in place. This begins with advice from a trusted team of professionals, including not only your broker executive but your CPA, lawyer, and other advisors. You should also include any business or family stakeholders who would be directly impacted by the documents. Lean on this group to make sure the documents you sign accurately reflect what everyone understands is the strategy.

Below are examples of some of the documents you may need, and brief descriptions of how they can be used to support your plan.

Will – Your Will legally records your intentions to transfer your estate to individuals or organizations. This is a smart document for anyone to have, but it can also be used to help communicate parts of your succession plan.

Buy-Sell Agreement – You can use a Buy-Sell Agreement to document events (such as death, disability, or retirement) that trigger a transfer in ownership of the business to your successors and how to fund that transfer. The document may refer to an "Entity Purchase," where the company owns the life insurance, or a "Cross Purchase," where partners own insurance on each other's lives.

Trust – A trust is a legal entity that can hold, protect, and distribute assets. It can be used to keep insurance proceeds outside of an owner's estate. This helps protect your assets, particularly in the case of unanticipated legal or health issues.

Life Insurance Policy – As mentioned above, this can fund the implementation of your succession plan at the time it is needed, even including a buy-out of an owner. It is not subject to income tax, and, with proper planning, may not be subject to estate tax either.

QUESTIONS TO ASK YOUR BROKER:

- What kind of succession planning have you done before? Have you done it for a circumstance similar to mine?

- Do you charge any fees to help me with succession planning?

- Do you have a vested interest in a particular insurance company, or can you independently assess my options for funding?

- Can you provide me with some sample documents to review in advance of our meeting?

QUESTIONS YOUR BROKER SHOULD ASK:

- Who are you trying to protect in this process? Your family, your business, your business partners, or some combination?

- What have you done so far? Do you have a will, a life insurance policy, or any other legal documents in place for your business?

- Do you, your business partners, your spouse or dependents have any existing medical issues that could impact this process?

- Can you provide me with contact information for advisors you have such as an attorney, CPA, or others?

- Are you depending on your business to be a source of funding for your retirement?

NOTES

CHAPTER 6
Use insurance to retain key personnel and protect your business

So, how do you keep things running if the leadership team doesn't make it back from their volcano-top retreat? Or, in a more likely scenario, can you use insurance to help keep your top salesman from jumping ship to a competitor?

Key personnel are any employees essential to your business. Specifically, they are essential enough to justify the purchase of either incentives that encourage them to remain with your company or protections for the business in the case of their disability or death. They can be a major sales generator, an executive overseeing an important business function, or even someone with enough proprietary knowledge to make them critical to keep around. They may just be someone with unique credentials or training that helps your business stand apart from your competition.

The bottom line is that these personnel have value to

your company, value that probably deserves to be protected. Consider the amount of revenue that depends on them, and the cost of finding and training

> *"... these personnel have value to your company, value that probably deserves to be protected."*

a replacement. For executives, note that this number is often 400% of the current annual salary. Small business leaders may also be particularly valuable because of the high-reliance of the company's success on their performance.

This value can be protected with insurance. Mechanisms that broker executives often use for this purpose are: disability insurance, long-term care insurance, and life insurance. These mechanisms can provide funds to the company to mitigate serious injury or death and be a valuable reward to the key employee. For the employee, it not only provides direct benefits but increased loyalty to the company, something often referred to as "golden handcuffs."

Disability Insurance

Disability insurance is generally available to your employees through their normal health plan. This plan can be expanded and enhanced for your key executives.

However, if you purchase the benefit through the business, pay attention to the tax implications. For instance, the purchase is tax-deductible to the business but the benefits are taxable to the employee. It may be better to have the business supplement the employee with additional income to cover any additional taxes to the employee, making the disability benefit tax-free for them to receive later.

You can also purchase "overhead disability." This is disability insurance on key employees, or even the owner(s), that yields funds to the business in the event that the employee becomes fully disabled. This can be especially valuable to a small business where the key executive is performing essential functions for the company, like generating a significant portion of the sales revenue. It's a benefit that can be used to cover salaries and other overhead cost for months or even years.

Long-Term Care Insurance

Long-Term Care (LTC) insurance can also be used as a benefit to key employees. As mentioned in Chapter 1, this is a very useful form of insurance that they're likely to need at some point. LTC insurance premiums can be tax-deductible for your business to purchase and tax-free for the individual when they need it. You can buy this as a standalone policy, or you can include it as a rider on a life

> *"... premiums can be tax-deductible for your business to purchase and tax-free for the individual when they need it."*

insurance policy. Ask your broker if it's more advantageous to provide this benefit to only a few, key persons, such as a "carve out" plan, or to offer it to all of your employees.

Life Insurance

Aside from direct compensation, life insurance may be one of the best ways to incentivize key personnel and to protect your business against their loss. Life insurance is relatively inexpensive, offers peace of mind to the employee, has tax advantages for both the company and the employee, and can be used to supplement the employee's retirement. And as you've no doubt come to understand through reading the other chapters in this book, there is no shortage of options available. Below are several examples of ways to consider structuring life insurance for key personnel:

- Fund life insurance policies for key personnel through the business. This is one example of an executive perk that could help with retention.

- Fund the policies through the business, but keep ownership with the business until the key personnel retire. This gives them an executive perk but motivates them to remain with the company until retirement to receive the benefits of the contract.

- Partially fund each policy, sharing or splitting the cost. This creates an executive perk and motivation for them to stay, but it costs less upfront to the company. It also gives key personnel the chance to take over the policy on their own, at their own cost, if they leave early.

- Incrementally fund each policy over time, with an agreement to cover the remainder of the cost at, or just before, retirement. This gives the perk and costs the least amount to the company over time, but it may not be a significant motivator to the employee since they could take over the payments at any time to retain the benefit.

The list above is not all-inclusive, nor does it cover all of the tax implications of these strategies. You can use life insurance to provide a unique source of retirement money, make the company a partial beneficiary until the

"Lay out your goals clearly with your broker executive and let them help you make the right decision for your business."

employee retires, withdraw cash on a schedule to minimize tax implications, or many other creative possibilities. Lay out your goals clearly with your broker executive and let them help you make the right decision for your business.

QUESTIONS TO ASK YOUR BROKER:

- What is the cost of insurance for key executives?

- What exactly are the benefits to the business? To the employee?

- How does this impact taxes? Are the payments deductible to the business or to the employee? What about the benefits?

- What kind of service do you provide regarding my policies? Will you give me an assessment of each policy at least once a year and meet to discuss it?

- Can you lay out several of the better options for my budget, so that we can limit the number of choices?

QUESTIONS YOUR BROKER SHOULD ASK:

- What monetary value do your identified key personnel provide to your business?

- What do you estimate is the cost of recruiting and training a replacement key person?

- Do you think your key personnel would respond better to your guaranteeing a small benefit in the near term or to a large benefit for staying loyal until retirement? Is the answer different for different employees?

- Have you already considered the different ways to mitigate the loss of each key member outside of insurance? What is your current strategy?

- Have you consulted with an attorney or CPA that recommended speaking to an insurance broker?

CHAPTER 7
Turn your broker into a broker executive, or find one.

In the past, business owners and their insurance brokers could all count on company customer service representatives to handle a wide range of issues, from bank account changes to investigating lapsed contract reinstatement requirements.

Now, the gradual downsizing of these companies has resulted in leaner, and less experienced, customer service organizations. Too often, they rely on scripted responses and automated systems to answer client needs. Some companies don't even send out an annual report except upon request. Broker executives take up this slack through closer monitoring, better

"Broker executives take up this slack through closer monitoring, better understanding of company offerings and systems, and even direct facilitation of conversations between their customers and the company."

understanding of company offerings and systems, and even direct facilitation of conversations between their customers and the company.

But before you go tossing your insurance agent out into the cold night to trade "up" to someone better, ask yourself if you've requested the service that you need. Many insurance agents and independent brokers face a lot of pressure from the companies they represent, other brokers, and customers like you to give only the simplest sales presentations. They may have the knowledge and experience you need, but if you've already made it clear that you only want the fastest, cheapest option, then that's exactly what they're going to give you. Rarely will you find someone that says, "No, I'd like to be sure you've considered all your options before you write any checks."

Yes, it's your broker's job to make finding insurance simpler, but you have a mutual responsibility to make sure they know what you really need. If they're jumping straight to the online quote generator, slow them down and ask hard questions. You can even give physical clues like setting your phone down and taking your jacket off. These are important decisions that are worth the time it takes to get them right.

But how do you know if you've already got a broker

executive? And if not, where can you get one?

Do I have a broker executive?

Effectively, there are two kinds of insurance agents: captive and independent. With some exceptions, captive agents work only for a single company and, while that company may have a wide variety of options, the captive agent is limited to selling to you only what their company offers. Independent agents, on the other hand, have a broader span of alternatives. They work to represent you and to help you compare options from multiple insurance companies. Independent agents are often referred to as insurance brokers.

Both captive and independent agents have their benefits and drawbacks. Captive agents understand their company's products and strategies, which may or may not meet your needs. If a captive agent is willing to say "this doesn't sound like the right policy for you," they may sincerely have your best interests in mind. As long as they aren't guiding you to a pre-constructed solution without first understanding what you really need, their professional opinion should be considered. Independent insurance brokers, on the other hand, can scan the whole range of options available to find the best offerings from many companies.

A captive agent, for example, may be able to offer you a simplified process and a system of employees familiar with ways to expedite your application. Independent agents, as you might expect, can also have financial advantage because of the different types of insurance they can consider. They also understand some of the loopholes and policy nuances that a captive agent wouldn't have any reason to explain.

What you're really looking for is someone with experience, credentials, and integrity. They are a professional financial consultant looking out for your best interest. Look for signs that they are asking questions to get to know you rather than to fill out fields on an application. See if they're following your signals as to the type of transaction you want, or if they're hurrying toward a select group of familiar options.

> *"What you're really looking for is someone with experience, credentials, and integrity. They are a professional financial consultant looking out for your best interest."*

Below are some simple questions you can ask yourself to determine if you already have a broker executive:

1. Are they speaking in terms of a long-term customer relationship?

2. Do their questions help me think through my real objectives?

3. Do they appear patient, interested, and focused only on me while we talk?

4. Are they helping me understand the risks and benefits of policies from different companies without bias?

5. Are they presenting options to me clearly, and taking the time to make sure I understand them?

6. Do they speak in terms of recent trends and how they might impact the options being discussed?

7. Are they really hearing the challenges I'm describing, and are they adjusting their questions appropriately as they listen?

Where do I find one?

So, you've patiently worked with your agent, pushed them to find you other options, asked hard questions, and given them the benefit of every doubt. If they aren't a broker executive with the commitment to look out for your best interests, it may be time to search for

"If they aren't a broker executive with the commitment to look out for your best interests, it may be time to search for someone else."

someone else.

Unfortunately, there isn't a directory of broker executives. There are only agents and brokers with a wide range of experience and motivation. You may want to start by searching your local area for independent brokers or independent agents with active memberships in professional organizations such as the Society of Financial Services Professionals (SFSP), Certified Financial Planners (CFP), and Estate Planning Council (EPC). Designations such as Certified Life Underwriter (CLU) and Chartered Financial Consultant (ChFC) are a couple of the certifications common to professional development for life insurance agents and brokers. You could start online or follow-up on recommendations from your CPA, attorney, or a respected colleague. They may work at small agencies or large firms, but they have in common a drive to know their business for their customer's sake.

Once you've got some ideas about which agents to talk to, call them and interview them. Think of them as a potential new asset to your business, one that will add value and not create risk. Below are some of the relevant criteria to consider in these discussions:

- *Credentials* – What certifications, education, and awards do they have? Are these standard in their field, or unique?

- *Customer Focus* – Are they responsive to your questions? Or are they more focused on getting an immediate sale?
- *Knowledge and Experience* – Have they been doing this for several years or more, and do they have the support of an experienced team? Do they speak confidently of their ability to find what's best for you?
- *Flexible Process* – What is their process for finding the right insurance? Do they start with a solution in mind, or are they asking questions to understand your needs?
- *Proactive Intentions* – Do they offer recommendations, and will they periodically review your policies, including current and future benefits?
- *Range of Options* – How many life insurance providers are they appointed with through the state insurance commissioner's office? Do you recognize the names and integrity of the companies they identify?
- *Attitude* – Are they willing to challenge your assumptions? Do they respond confidently and ask pointed questions in return? Are you comfortable with their tone, pace, and style of conversation?

There are good companies and contracts out there,

and there are insurance brokers willing and able to help you find them. But, the insurance business isn't getting simpler, and the value of having a broker executive is increasingly important. Make a broker executive part of your executive team to minimize your cost, limit your risk, and maximize protection for yourself and your business.

"Make a broker executive part of your executive team to minimize your cost, limit your risk, and maximize protection for yourself and your business."

A NOTE FROM THE AUTHOR

My father, Val senior, started the Vogel Insurance agency the same year I was born, in 1955. His enthusiasm for his insurance business was an inspiration to me growing up; and to this day, he remains a dynamic and motivating individual. It was a business built on the values of integrity and exceptional customer service, values that were the foundation of what became a life-long successful insurance business for him.

I didn't join his business immediately, however. After college, my wife Michelle and I decided to take on a new adventure to become "houseparents" for a children's home in Illinois through a volunteer program. After a couple years had passed and I had a new Masters Degree in Social Work, we decided to return home to New Orleans for me to take a newly vacated position at my father's firm. Ten years later in 1991, I co-founded my current business, Burns, Vogel and Associates. Our goals are still very much in line with my fathers, constantly looking for better ways to provide value to our customers and other agents we work with.

I wrote Broker Executive to capture and share what I believe are essential elements of being a great insurance broker. My team and I respect our customers enough to help them make informed decisions. We care for them enough to look for insurance solutions that meet their needs. And we know our mutual trust will lend itself to repeat business and referrals. I hope you saw these elements throughout this book, and I hope even more that you'll find the integrity and dedication you deserve from the brokers you know.

Val

To learn about Val's business and their services,
please visit: **www.BurnsVogel.com**

To find more great books from this publisher,
please visit: **www.AECStellar.com**

If you enjoyed this book,
please take a moment to place a review online.

This is the best way to support a writer – either by sharing
your praise with other readers, or by providing your fair
perspective on ways the author can grow and improve.

Thank you!

www.ingramcontent.com/pod-product-compliance
Lightning Source LLC
Chambersburg PA
CBHW050529190326

41458CB00045B/6767/J

* 9 7 8 0 9 8 9 3 1 2 8 2 0 *